MY AMERICAN GIRL DOl
Superheroes Fighting
Bullying with Kindness

WRITTEN BY
CARLA ANDREA AND LOLO SMITH

Text by Carla Andrea and LoLo Smith ©2016
Photography by Tep Gardner
Illustrations/Graphics: Total Entertainment Package

Printed in the United States of America

All Rights Reserved.

Published by:
Do The Write Thing Foundation of DC
56 T Street, NW
Washington, DC 20001
202.518.1084 or 202.239.8293
Email: dothewritething1@gmail.com
Website: dothewritethingdc.com

American Girl is a trademark of American Girl corporation, a wholly owned subsidiary of Mattel. Reference to the American Girl doll is for the
information and convenience of the public and does not constitute endorsement or recommendation by the American Girl corporation. The
American Girl corporation was not involved in any way with the writing, design or publication of this book.

DEDICATION

To
Ghada Veronica Norde'
Gia Swann Norde'
Rian Lawrence
Madison Turell
Kassidy White
Imari-Sky Charles
Dakiyah Simmons
Deanna Lucas
Maleah DuBois

With special thanks to:
Cleopatra Jones, Neighbors of Seaton Place
Madiana Margao, Red Sprinkle
Antoine Anderson, Mini M.E. Children Models
Anthony Morton, Malcolm X Opportunity Center

Supergirl wants you to learn about bullying. She wants you to have a plan to stop bullying because bullying is not okay.

Batgirl says that bullying can happen anywhere. So beware!

2

The Girl Flash says that bullying can happen at home, at school, on the playground and even on the internet.

This is the Invisible Woman from the Fantastic Four. She says there are four types of bullying:

1. Verbal bullying
2. Physical bullying
3. Social bullying
4. Cyber bullying

4

Here is Elastigirl and Violet from the Incredibles. They say that verbal bullying happens when a bully says unkind things to someone or about someone. A bully may also call you names. Bullying is not the same as friendly teasing.

5

This is the Captain America Girl. She says that physical bullying means hitting, spitting, kicking, pinching or throwing things.

Spidergirl says social bullying means leaving others out on purpose, spreading rumors or telling others not to be friends with someone.

Wonder Woman teaches us about cyber bullying. She says to remember to always use kind words on the internet. Don't be mean behind the computer screen!

Robin teaches us that there are four roles that people play in a bullying situation:

1. The bully
2. The victim
3. The ally
4. The bystander

The Green Lantern Girl says that a bully is someone who tries to hurt others. Bullies feel better by doing unkind things. Bullies think they are cool. Bullies are not cool. Be a buddy, not a bully.

The She Hulk says that the victim of bullying is someone who is being called names, being hit or being left out. A victim may have trouble sleeping, stop doing their work at school, become sad, become afraid or even want to stop living.

This Girl Teenage Mutant Ninja Turtle says that a victim can be any color, size or age. It is okay to be different. It is not okay to bully someone for being different.

This Girl Teenage Mutant Ninja Turtle says that the ally is a friend of the bully. The ally is happy to see the bully hurt others.

This Girl Teenage Mutant Ninja Turtle says that bystanders do nothing to help a victim of bullying. That is wrong.

The Girl Teenage Mutant Ninja Turtle says you should help a victim by telling an adult. If you see something, say something. This is not tattling.

Girl Captain America says you can stop being a victim by laughing at the bully. Ha, ha, ha, ha.

Violet of the Incredibles, says you can just ignore a bully and walk away.

Green Lantern Girl says that you should ask a bully to stop. If the bully does not stop, you should tell your parent or your teacher.

Batgirl wants you to BE A BUDDY, NOT A BULLY.
Batgirl says IF YOU SEE SOMETHING, SAY SOMETHING.
Batgirl wants you to sign the pledge to STAND UP AGAINST
BULLYING LIKE A SUPERHERO.

19

I PLEDGE TO SAY NO TO BULLYING

☐ I pledge to stop bullying my sister or brother at home.

☐ I pledge to stop bullying other children at school.

☐ I pledge to stop bullying other children on the playground.

☐ I pledge to stop bullying on the Internet.

☐ I pledge to tell an adult when I see someone being bullied.

☐ I pledge to say no to bullying and be like a superhero.

_____
Name

(COPY THIS PLEDGE ON A SHEET OF PAPER)

10
Acts Of Kindness

The superheroes fight bullying with kindness.

When children act kind to one another, bullying decreases in schools.

It does not cost anything to be kind.

On the next 10 pages are 10 acts of kindness to try at home with your parents.

Act Of Kindness #1

Use sidewalk chalk and write kind messages on the sidewalk or parking lot in your neighborhood.

22

A warm smile is the universal language of kindness.

Act Of Kindness #2

Think of three relatives that you do not see very often. Write a nice, handwritten letter or card and drop it in the mail. Your letter or card will make them smile because it is rare to get a handwritten letter since most people just send texts or email.

We rise by lifting others.

Act Of Kindness #3

The next time you are in a car, wave and smile at people in other cars to see if they will wave or smile back at you.

Kindness is free.

24

Act Of Kindness #4

Take flowers to your favorite teacher. They are much better than apples!

"Never look down on someone unless you are helping them up."
-Jesse Jackson

Act Of Kindness #5

If you have an elderly neighbor, check in on them and ask if you can be of any help.

No act of kindness, no matter how small, is ever wasted.

26

Act Of Kindness #6

Share a special toy with a friend.

Choose kindness.

Act Of Kindness #7

Ask a parent if they will take you to the children's hospital so you can donate your gently used toys.

Children's Hospital

Kindness is always in season.

Act Of Kindness #8

Make a thank you card for your teacher or principal.

thank you!

thank you!

thank you!

One kind word can change someone's entire day.

Act Of Kindness #9

Read a book to a younger sister or brother.

Kindness is the language which the deaf can hear and the blind can see.

Invite a classmate who is easily left out, to play on the playground.

It's cool to be kind.

THE KINDNESS PLEDGE

☐ I pledge to be kind to my family at home.

☐ I pledge to be kind to my classmates at school.

☐ I pledge to be kind to my classmates on the playground.

☐ I pledge to be kind to others on the Internet.

☐ I pledge to tell an adult when I see someone being unkind.

☐ I pledge to be a buddy, not a bully.

☐ I pledge to be just like a superhero by fighting bullying with kindness.

_____
Name

(COPY THIS PLEDGE ON A SHEET OF PAPER)

ABOUT THE AUTHORS

CARLA ANDREA was born and raised in the District of Columbia. After graduating from Wilson Senior High School, she worked for several years then matriculated at Trinity University for three years. She now provides consulting services to non-profits that use the arts to enhance the life success of children and youth. She is the single mother of two children, a son and daughter. She wrote this book in response to her son being bullied at school. Carla has written two other pro-kindness, bullying prevention books: *Stand Up Against Bullying Like A Superhero* and *Superheroes Fight Bullying with Kindness*.

LoLo Smith is an educator, writer and creator of Living Storybook, a literacy program for young children. She has written three other books, *Mr. Jordan Goes To Washington, I Know My Community Workers* and *Sista Cindy Ella Mae*, the African-American re-telling of the Cinderella story. She was raised and educated in St. Louis but has lived in Washington, D.C. for over forty years. She has one adult son.

ABOUT THE PHOTOGRAPHER/GRAPHIC DESIGNER

Tep Gardner is an award winning entertainment photographer with over 40 years of experience. He is a green screen photography expert who specializes in iportraits, special events and fashion shoots. He has prvided photographic coverage for numerous corporations and national events. Contact him at:

202-239-0643

e-mail: tep@totalentertainmentpackage.com.

Visit his website at www.TotalEntertainmentPackage.com